"DOGS BELIEVE THEY ARE HUMAN. CATS BELIEVE THEY ARE GOD."

JEFF VALDEZ

INSTA GRAMMAR
JUST CATS

LANNOO

@FATCATART

@FATCATART

@FATCATART

@FATCATART

@FLUFFY_NERFS

@FLUFFY_NERFS

“IT IS IMPOSSIBLE TO KEEP A STRAIGHT FACE IN THE PRESENCE OF ONE OR MORE KITTENS.”

CYNTHIA E. VARNADO

@FLUFFY_NERFS

@FLUFFY_NERFS

@KARLIJNEG

@KARLIJNEG

@KARLIJNEG

@KARLIJNEG

@LEO.MAINECOON

@LEO.MAINECOON

@MAINECOONQUEENS

“IF CATS COULD TALK, THEY WOULDN’T.”

NAN PORTER

@HAMZA_H_DJENAT

@HAMZA_H_DJENAT

@METATRONEYES_MAINE_COONS

@PRINCESSCHEETO

@PRINCESSCHEETO

@PRINCESSCHEETO

@PRINCESSCHEETO

@PRINCESSCHEETO

@PRINCESSCHEETO

@THEBIRMANTWINS

@THEBIRMANTWINS

@THEBIRMANTWINS

@THEBIRMANTWINS

“CATS
HAVE IT ALL.
ADMIRATION,
AN ENDLESS
SLEEP, AND
COMPANY ONLY
WHEN THEY
WANT IT.”

ROD MCKUEN

@THIS_IS_AICO

@WOLFIE_THE_BRITISHSHORTHAIR

@WOLFIE_THE_BRITISHSHORTHAIR

@EVERYTHING_ABOUTCATS_

@EVERYTHING_ABOUTCATS_

@EVERYTHING_ABOUTCATS_

@EVERYTHING_ABOUTCATS_

@LYO.THECAT

@LYO.THECAT

@LITTLELORDREGINALD

@LITTLELORDREGINALD

@LYO.THECAT

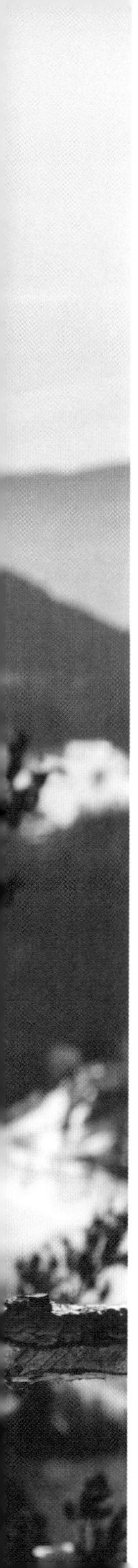

@LYO.THECAT

@AMY_SIMBA

@AMY_SIMBA

@AMY_SIMBA

@AMY_SIMBA

@AMY_SIMBA

"IT ALWAYS GIVES ME A SHIVER WHEN I SEE A CAT SEEING WHAT I CAN'T SEE."

ELEANOR FARJEON

@HOSICO_CAT

@HOSICO_CAT

@HOSICO_CAT

HOSICO_CAT

@KATH88KATH

@KATH88KATH

@TACHINEKO.YM

@TACHINEKO.YM

@TACHINEKO.YM

“SOMETIMES THEY JUST APPEAR IN YOUR LIFE, CATS.”

RON CURRIE JR

@TACHINEKOYM

@GUNBATIMINDAKIMOR

@GUNBATIMINDAKIMOR

@YOSHINORI_MIZUTANI

@YOSHINORI_MIZUTANI

@SLY.GATO

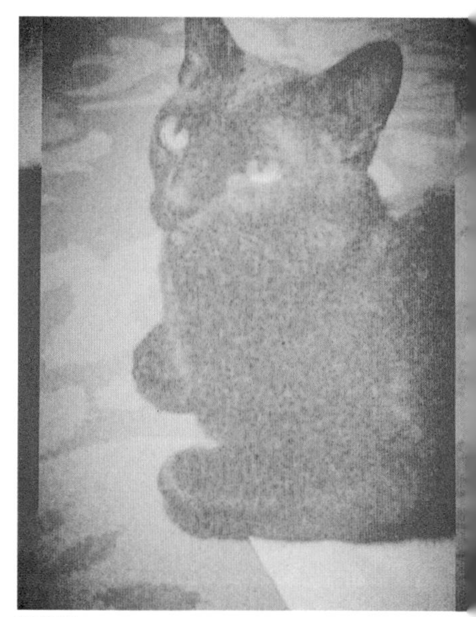
@SLY.GATO

LY.GATO

@SLY.GATO

@SLY.GATO

@PRIMUSCAT

“MY CAT IS NOT INSANE, SHE’S JUST A REALLY GOOD ACTRESS.”

P.C. CAST

@PRIMUSCAT

@PRIMUSCAT

@PRIMUSCAT

@PRIMUSCAT

@SKY.CATTERY

@SKY.CATTERY

@SKY.CATTERY

@SKY.CATTERY

@SKY.CATTERY

@THESEY_CAT

@THESEY_CAT

@THESEY_CAT

@THESEY_CAT

@EVERYDAY_OLIVE

@EVERYDAY_OLIVE

@KUROTOINU

@KUROTOINU

@KUROTOINU

@KUROTOINU

@KUROTOINU

@NYAJI100

@NYAJI100

@NYAJI100

@ROLLO_SHOEGAZER

@ROLLO_SHOEGAZER

@ZEN_REN_SEN_SIN

@ZEN_REN_SEN_SIN

@ZEN_REN_SEN_SIN

@ZEN_REN_SEN_SIN

“IF A CAT SPOKE, IT WOULD SAY THINGS LIKE ‘HEY, I DON’T SEE THE PROBLEM HERE.’”

ROY BLOUNT JR

@ZEN_REN_SEN_SIN

@ZEN_REN_SEN_SIN

“NO, I
NEVER
THOUGHT
I WOULD
LIKE
CATS”

KARL LAGERFELD

MARKED is an initiative by Lannoo Publishers
www.markedbylannoo.com

Sign up for our MARKED newsletter with news about new and forthcoming publications on art, interior design, food & travel, photography and fashion as well as exclusive offers and events.

Photo Selection/Book Design: Irene Schampaert

Cover Image: @lyo.thecat

Also available:
Insta Grammar Cats
Insta Grammar City
Insta Grammar Nordic
Insta Grammar Dogs
Insta Grammar Green
Insta Grammar Graphic
Insta Grammar Unicorn
Insta Grammar Cars
Insta Grammar Love
Insta Grammar On the Road

If you have any questions or comments about the material in this book, please do not hesitate to contact our editorial team: markedteam@lannoo.com

© Lannoo Publishers, Tielt, Belgium, 2020
D/2020/45/169 – NUR 652/653
ISBN: 9789401463485
www.lannoo.com

All rights reserved. No part of this publication may be reproduced or transmitted in any form or by any means, electronic or mechanical, including photocopy, recording or any other information storage and retrieval system, without prior permission in writing from the publisher.

Every effort has been made to trace copyright holders. If, however, you feel that you have inadvertently been overlooked, please contact the publishers.

#AREYOUMARKED